SEED SAVING FOR
BEGINNERS

The Comprehensive Guide to Harvesting, Drying and Storing Healthy Seeds with Easy to Follow Steps

Kevin R. Smith

Table of Contents

Introduction

Saving seeds is a traditional technique that enables farmers and gardeners to maintain genetic diversity, take charge of their own food supply, and safeguard our agricultural legacy. Seed saving assumes particular significance in British gardens, where it enables the cultivation and propagation of historic types that have been handed down through the years.

Preserving genetic variety is one of the main motivations for seed storage. Preserving seeds guarantees that lesser-known, regional variants do not vanish in a world where a small number of commercially available seed varieties control the majority of the market. Many times, the distinctive flavors, colors, and characteristics of these heirloom and heritage seeds have been lost during the commercialization process. We honor our agricultural and cultural heritage and stay connected to our roots by keeping these seeds.

Furthermore, by preserving seeds, we can develop plants that are suited to our particular growing environment. Seeds gathered from plants that have long flourished in a particular area are highly adapted to the temperature, soil, and pests of that area. Compared to generic commercial types, these seeds are more durable and productive because they possess the genetic characteristics that have allowed them to thrive in the area. Replanting and preserving locally appropriate seeds will help us create a self-sufficient food system that requires fewer outside resources.

Additionally, seed saving encourages self-sufficiency and food security. We can lessen our reliance on seed businesses and guarantee a wide variety of crops for upcoming generations by preserving and exchanging seeds within our communities. We are less susceptible to disruptions in the global food supply chain when we are able to cultivate our own food from preserved seeds. Although it is reasonably simple to begin, storing seeds does require some expertise and careful attention to detail. The first step is to choose open-pollinated plants, which give rise to progeny that bear striking resemblances to their parents. Because their genetic makeup doesn't change over many generations, these plants are perfect for seed preservation. It's critical to harvest the seeds at the appropriate period when the plants mature. Whether it is gathering the seeds from the fruit or waiting for the seed pods to dry, every plant has its own set of rules when it comes to gathering seeds.

You are about to go on a trip that goes beyond the basic act of planting and harvesting on the pages that follow. You will learn about the deep significance of seeds—the silent life-bearers that provide us with sustenance in the present, link us to the past, and hold the key to a prosperous future.

The practice of saving seeds has become a ray of hope in an era of rapidly changing environmental conditions and declining genetic diversity. It offers a practical means for people to take back control of their food supply, maintain traditional knowledge, and protect the priceless genetic resources that are essential to all life.

In "Seed Saving For Beginners," we will examine the basic ideas, methods, and morality of seed saving, giving you the information and self-assurance to start your own seed-saving endeavor. This book is your comprehensive guide to solving the riddles of seed preservation and maximizing its transforming potential, regardless of your level of experience as a farmer or gardener—whether you're a beginner with a few pots on your balcony or a seasoned pro with acres of land under cultivation.

You will find information on how to choose the best seeds, check for viability, and store them for later use throughout these pages. You'll learn the finer points of cross-breeding and pollination, as well as how to keep your seed supplies pure and stop unintended genetic drift. Armed with doable fixes and tried-and-true tactics passed down through the generations of seed savers, you will face typical obstacles and disappointments head-on.

Come along with me as we go off on this path of empowerment, adventure, and discovery. Let us tend not only vibrant gardens but also communities bound together by a common respect for the wonder of seeds. One harvest, one seed at a time.

Chapter One

Explanation of what Seed Saving is and Why it's important.

Seed Saving is an age-old method of seed keeping. It involves Gathering and preserving plant seeds for future use. The process entails the intentional selection of plants possessing desired characteristics, letting them to maturity, collecting the seeds, and preserving them in an ideal environment to guarantee their survival for subsequent plantings. Seed saving can be as easy as preserving the seeds from a tomato plant you love in your backyard garden or as difficult as running a farm with a large assortment of heirloom kinds.

What Makes Saving Seeds Important?

1.Genetic variation Preservation: One of the most important ways to protect genetic variation among plant species is through seed storage. A great deal of traditional fruit, vegetable, and grain varieties have disappeared or are in danger of going extinct due to industrial agriculture and the growth of  monoculture crops. Seed savers preserve a rich pool of genetic material that can be used to breed new kinds with desirable features like insect resistance, drought tolerance, and flavor by saving seeds from a variety of regionally suited and diversified plants.

2.Resilience in the Face of Environmental Change: Agricultural systems around the world are in danger of becoming unstable due to environmental issues such as habitat loss and climate change. Because different types may show varying degrees of adaptability to changing environments, diverse seed supplies provide resilience in the face of these difficulties. Seed savers help create resilient agricultural systems that can endure environmental pressures by preserving seeds from plants that flourish in specific microclimates and soil types.

3.Food Sovereignty and Food Security: Seed saving is a form of resistance, a strategy for people and communities to take control of their food supply, in a time of patented genetically modified seeds and corporate domination of the seed industry. Seed savers give communities more control over the kinds of crops they cultivate and eat by preserving and exchanging seeds locally, which lessens reliance on outside seed suppliers. By conserving customary knowledge and dietary practices that have been passed down through the centuries, seed preservation also fosters cultural resilience.

4.Financial Gains for Farmers and Gardeners: By lowering the annual seed purchase requirement, seed saving can provide financial gains for farmers and gardeners. Seed savers can create self-sustaining seed stocks tailored to their unique growing conditions, thereby reducing their reliance on commercial seed providers. Seed saving also promotes a deeper connection to the soil and a better awareness of the natural cycles of plant growth and reproduction.

To sum up, the traditional practice of storing seeds has significant consequences for the preservation of biodiversity, food security, cultural heritage, and community resilience. By saving seeds, people actively contribute to preserving our agricultural heritage and creating a more equitable and sustainable food system for future generations.

Chapter 2

Understanding Seeds

Anatomy of a Seed

Among the most significant and intriguing achievements of the botanical world are seeds. They are, after all, the culmination of all plants that produce seeds; their lifetime investment, carefully crafted to guarantee the survival of the following generation.

Even though they are available in every conceivable combination of sizes, colors, shapes, and forms, seeds all have an ancient anatomy that goes back hundreds of millions of years.

The basic structural components of all seeds are the same, even if each plant has its own methods for producing seeds. They're:

the three parts of a seed

1.Seed Coat: is the hard tissue enclosing the seed.

2. Embryo.The tissues that give rise to the plant's future branches, leaves. The cotyledons are a part of this also.

3. Endosperm: is a storage organ present in a wide variety of plants, especially monocots.

1.Seed Coat

The outer covering of the seed, known as the seed coat, serves as both protection and a mediator for a number of critical processes involved in germination and dormancy. It's the portion of the seed that is visible to us when we examine it; it can have a range of colors and textures as well as thickness and smoothness.

While they are often semi-permeable, they are made to keep bacteria, fungi, or viruses out of the plant and threaten its future health. Dormancy shields the interior structures from pests and possible predators. By keeping the nutrients unavailable while they move through an animal's digestive tract or by preventing predators from breaking them open for food, thick seed coverings can deter predators from accessing the nutrient-rich insides. Similarly, the seeds' protection in the animal's digestive tract aids in their dissemination when they land in the nutrient-rich excrement of the animal.

The proper timing of seed germination is also mediated by seed coverings. Fire-dependent seeds, for instance, have thick seed coats that only split open in the presence of high heat. This guarantees that in the wake of a wildfire, they will grow with minimal competition. Certain light waves can penetrate the thin seed coverings of some seeds that germinate whether or not sunlight is present.

The Seed Coat Components (3 parts)

- Testa: The majority of the seed coat is composed of this outer layer of the seed. It is the seed coat's thick layer of defense.

- Tegmen: The layer that lies below the testa and above the seed's interior is thinner than the surrounding tissue. Water can enter more easily through a micropyle, which is a tiny pore. On some seed coats, it is frequently apparent.

- Hilum: The place where the seed was affixed to the remainder of the fruit is shown by this little "scar" on the seed coat.

2. The Embryo (connection to the chicks here)

The embryo, which is likely the most significant component of the seed, is located beneath the seed coat. The purpose of every other portion of the seed is to safeguard and guarantee the embryo's survival. The reason for this is that it comprises the basic tissues that will eventually give rise to all other plant sections. These embryonic cells gave rise to all of the leaves and roots you see on a fully grown plant.

There are four main structural components of an embryo:

- Cotyledon: In many seeds, the cotyledons make up the majority of the bulk and volume. Grass is a monocot, whereas beans and tomatoes are dicots, which have one cotyledon. During germination, the developing seed has to be fed, and the cotyledons serve as stores of nutrients and energy. Cotyledons are raised above the ground in many plant species, allowing them to carry out photosynthesis and aid in the growth of the plant. Cotyledons in other plants remain underground and provide nourishment to the developing plants.

  essentially the seed's fridge

- Hypocotyl and Epicotyl: A developing seedling's epicotyl and hypocotyl are stem tissues that are situated on either side of the cotyledons. Positioned under the cotyledons, the hypocotyl is attached to the embryonic

  becomes stem

root below. Supporting the plumule, the epicotyl is situated just above the cotyledons.

- Plumule: The name plumule, derived from the Latin word pluma, which means feather, refers to the structure that is situated at the tip of the epicotyl and frequently resembles a tiny feather-like structure. The tissues contain the meristems that eventually give rise to all of the plant's branches and leaves. Generally speaking, the epicotyl is where all of the above-ground tissues in a plant begin.

- Radicle: The radicle, sometimes referred to as the embryonic root, is the first root to grow out of a growing seed. Anchoring the seed into the earth is its primary function, and it frequently expands to a comparatively great size. After the radicle is in the soil, it starts to grow root hairs that may take up nutrients and water. A huge tap root that searches for nutrients below ground and provides the plant with deep anchoring is formed by the radicle in certain plants.

3. The Endosperm

A developing embryo's storage organ, the endosperm is found in the seeds of many flowering plants. It is mostly made up of carbs, but it also has lipids, minerals, and all the other components required for growth. Their function and frequency differ significantly between dicots and monocots, even though they are present in the basic anatomy of all seeds.

Dicots: Dicots are plants having two cotyledons, such as beans, tomatoes, and mint. Although endosperms are present in dicots, they are generally underdeveloped in most species. The endosperm's function is replaced during the formation of these seeds by the rapid mobilization of nutrients from the endosperm to the cotyledons. As a result of having fully developed endosperms, some dicots are referred to as "endospermic dicots."

endosperm plays a stronger role in these plants/seeds

Monocot Endosperms: The anatomy of monocots depends heavily on endosperms. These include plants with only one cotyledon, such grasses and flowering plants that resemble grass. This encompasses all the real grains that humans eat, such as corn, wheat, and rye. Actually, the reason these grains are so valuable to our culture is because of the nutrients found in the endosperm.

Additional Seed Structure

Plants have evolved numerous inventive tactics to increase the chances of their seeds surviving since their creation some 400 million years ago. Certain plant lineages have produced numerous extra structures that aid in the protection or dissemination of seeds.

1.Burs: Prickly structures known as burs surround seeds and aid in their distribution. Hikers frequently have these burs become lodged in their shoes, socks, and trouser legs. They are also infamous for becoming tangled in dogs' fur.

2.Wings: These components enhance the seed's aerodynamic qualities. This makes it easier for the wind to disperse the seeds and extends their range. "Samaras" are seeds that have wings on them.

3.Fruits that are fleshy: Everyone has heard of this. Modified parts of the mother plants' previous ovaries are fleshy fruits. The seeds will spread to new areas thanks to their high nutrient content and ability to draw in animal dispersers.

4.Capsules : Before the seeds are ready to be released, the seeds are protected by the strong, dry capsules, which are specialized fruit structures.

5.The Elaiosome: is a unique structure that is rich in proteins and lipids and is affixed to the outside of seeds. While they serve a similar function to fleshy fruits, these are especially crucial for ant and other insect dissemination.

6.Pappus: The fluffy cotton inside dandelion seeds that aids in wind dispersal is known as pappus. Many members of the sunflower family contain it.

7.Mucilage: Around the seed coat of some seeds is a sticky membrane known as mucilaginous membrane. This can aid in dissemination by sticking to gullible animals when wet.

8.Trichomes: These tiny, crystal-like hairs have the ability to discourage herbivory or aid in dissemination.

Types of Seeds

Open-pollinated, Hybrid, Heirloom, and Genetically Modified Organisms (GMOs).

It takes more than just knowing what kind of plant you want to grow to choose the proper seeds. There are benefits and drawbacks to hybrid, open-pollinated, and heirloom seeds based on your unique requirements.

Open-pollinated Seed

Plants that receive their fertilization from the elements—such as pollinating insects, birds, rain, and wind—are the source of open-pollinated seeds. One of these techniques allows two plants of the same variety to cross-pollinate, producing a seed that matures into a plant that is nearly identical to the parent plants with very minor differences. The seeds are able to gradually adjust to the local climate because of the genetic variety that results from these differences.

Keep your plants apart from other types of the same species if you are preserving seeds from open-pollinated plants. Your open-pollinated plant will generate seeds with diverse features and may lose its advantageous traits if it crosses with a different variety of the same plant.

Hybrid Seed

In order to develop a hybrid with favorable qualities from each variety, plant breeders cross-polinate two plant varieties to produce hybrid seeds, a process called hybrid vigor. Plant breeders may, for instance, cross-breed a particularly hardy tomato plant with a disease-resistant tomato plant to produce a novel strain of disease-resistant and hardy tomato seed. In nature, cross-pollination might happen at random, but the hybrid seed kinds you can buy are intentionally created by people.

If you preserve seeds from that new batch of plants to grow the next season, it's a different story. First-generation hybrid plant seeds, also known as F1 hybrids, will provide larger yields of plants with the appropriate combination of features. It will take roughly seven generations for the seeds from these second-generation hybrid varieties, sometimes referred to as F2 hybrids, to yield a satisfactory harvest. Only a small percentage of these hybrid plants will be identical to the F1 hybrids. This is why people who grow hybrid plants buy fresh seeds every year instead of storing the seeds from their hybrid plants.

What's the difference between GMO and hybrid seeds?

When two distinct plant varieties cross-pollinate, hybrid seeds are produced. Observes that genetic engineering techniques such as gene splicing are used in laboratories to create genetically modified organisms, or GMOs. The majority of hybrid seeds available for purchase are not modified genetically. Since GMO seeds are usually only employed by large-scale commercial producers, amateur gardeners are unlikely to come across them while perusing a local garden center or seed catalog.

How Do Heirloom Seeds Differ?

Plants that are open to pollination are the source of heirloom seed kinds, which have a tradition of transmitting desirable characteristics from parent plants to offspring. These beneficial traits, which can include flavor, production, pest and disease resistance, hardiness, and climate adaptability, are established during many years of cultivation. In general, seeds from plant types that are at least fifty years old are required to qualify as heirloom varieties. Not all open-pollinated plants are heirloom plants, even though all heirloom seeds originate from these types.

Heirloom seeds have the following advantages over hybrid seeds:

They are less expensive, produce more tasty food than hybrid seeds, are climate-adapted, and always yield offspring true to their parent plant, so you can keep your seeds for next year's harvest.

Chapter 3

Choosing the Right Seeds to Save

You can keep the vegetable seeds from your backyard garden to sow again the following year. Choosing appropriate plants to save seeds from, harvesting seeds at the appropriate time, and storing them correctly over the winter are all part of seed saving.

Self Pollinating Plants *good seeds to start with*

Beans, peas, tomatoes, and peppers are excellent options for preserving seeds. They have self-pollinating blooms and seeds that need little to no special preparation before storage.

Given that biennial crops like beets and carrots require two growing seasons in order to set seed, saving their seeds is more difficult.

What good is this project if children are not also growing something

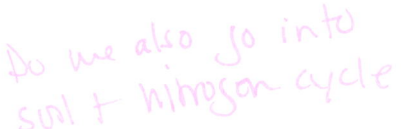
Do we also go into soil + nitrogen cycle

Cross Pollinated Plants

Cross-pollination can occur in plants like maize and vine crops that have distinct male and female flowers. Maintaining the pure strain of the seed is challenging.

On a windy day, popcorn can help pollinate a stand of sweet corn from a nearby garden. A crop generated from these seeds will not produce decent popcorn or sweet corn; this will impact the flavor of the current sweet corn harvest.

Gourds, cucumbers, melons, squash, and pumpkins can all be cross-pollinated by insects.

Seeds from such a hybrid will grow into vines with fruit that is different from that of the parent plant, but cross-pollination will not impact the quality of the current crop. This frequently leads to poorer flavor and other qualities.

Open Pollinated Plants

Go for open-pollinated kinds over hybrids when preserving seed. When open-pollinated cultivars self-pollinate or cross-pollinate with other cultivars of the same variety, the seed they produce grows into plants that bear striking similarities to the parent plant. These plants have similar-looking fruit and produce seeds that lead to the growth of other similar plants.

Certain types that pollinate freely could be considered "heirlooms." These cultivars are passed down through the centuries by gardeners, or they might be more modern selections.

There are tomato types that aren't hybrids. These include "Big Rainbow," "San Marzano," and "Brandywine," among other open-pollinated varieties. These types' seed will grow into plants that resemble their parent plants almost exactly, bearing fruit that is almost identical.

As with peppers, beans, and peas, open-pollinated types that bear fruit from seed include Habanero, California Wonder, and Corno di Toro; peas, Lincoln, Little Marvel, and Perfection; and beans, Kentucky Wonder, Blue Lake, and Textrcrop.

Following the planting of an open-pollinated crop,

- Decide which plants you wish to save their seeds from.
- Selecting the most robust plants with the best-tasting fruit to serve as parents for the following year's crop is important.
- Weak or off-type plants should not have their seed saved.

Hybrid Plants

Vegetable hybrid plants are the result of crossing two distinct kinds, combining characteristics from both parent plants. Sometimes a combination works especially well, resulting in plants with exceptional yield, disease resistance, and vigor. Because they are more expensive to produce, hybrid seeds are typically more expensive.

Some hybrid plants, including the tomatoes 'Big Boy, Beefmaster, and Early Girl,' can provide viable seed.

- The plants cultivated from that seed are not the same as the parents of the hybrid.

- They will be an entirely new fusion of the positive and negative characteristics of the original cross plants.

- It is hard to estimate the exact performance of the seedling plant or the kind of quantity the fruit will be.

Things to take into account while selecting plants for seed saving

Being able to order seeds annually is a relatively new concept in the history of agriculture. Seed saving was just a normal aspect of gardening for thousands of years. This family's legacy produced the heirlooms we recognize today and modified types to suit particular regional climates.

Every time we preserve seeds, we are making judgments on the morphology of plants for future generations. Selecting seeds to save for the following year requires thought. It could be tempting to plant leftovers or ingredients you don't want to use in cooking, especially when it comes to easily preserved species like potatoes or garlic, but keep in mind that this will have an impact on subsequent harvests. Check out some of the qualities to keep in mind when preserving seed.

Vigour

This is the capacity of a plant to germinate effectively and develop into a robust, fruitful plant soon.

Time of Day

Choosing for early output may be preferable, even if your season is rather long. Fast-maturing plants can help you harvest more than one crop, avoid specific pests, enjoy produce sooner in the growing season, and so on.

Accuracy to the type

When attempting to conserve an heirloom variety, you should make sure that the seeds you save come exclusively from plants that accurately represent the traits that make that variety special.

Illness and Insect Resistance

You can alter a variety to better tolerate local pests and illnesses by saving seed from year to year.

Tolerance for High or Drastic Moisture

Another method you might tailor a variety to your particular garden site is by using this characteristic.

Unpredictability

Often requiring extra trellising, tall, spindly plants might be susceptible to lodging and other issues. Plants that are stocky tend to be healthy ones. Keep in mind that plant spacing and fertilizer availability might also have an impact on this characteristic.

Hardiness

You should choose plants that can tolerate freezing conditions, especially for crops that are cultivated in the early spring or late fall.

Being tardy to Bolt

Don't save the seed from the first plants that drop their seeds. Your harvest season will be extended if you choose plants that bolt later.

Color

Even while it might not appear as significant as flavor or disease resistance, heirloom varieties are frequently chosen because of their distinctive color. Part of the uniqueness of the variety is picking the purest Purple Dragon Carrots.

Homogeneity or absence of it

Depending on your variety, this quality will vary. While you might like every one of your green arrow pea plants to be the same height, it goes without saying that you do not want your rainbow swiss chard to be the same color.

A taste

Heirlooms' incredible flavor is among their best qualities! This is something you should always keep in mind when storing seeds. Tasteless veggies don't have a place in life.

Flesh Features

This feature will mostly rely on the intended use of the variety. Slicers like Radiator Charlie's Mortgage Lifter should have a lot more moisture than tomatoes like Principe Borghese, which were designed for drying.

Form and Dimensions

Save the seeds from the largest peppers if you enjoy stuffed jalapenos. This is yet another excellent method for making variation work for you.

Efficiency of Work

Despite the allure, resist the want to consume your largest and best cabbages. So that in a few years more of your cabbages will resemble the greatest, let those go to seed.

Capacity to Store

Storage capacity should still be taken into consideration, especially in plants like storage tomatoes, pumpkins, winter squash, sweet potatoes, etc., even though it might appear less significant in the present world when everyone has a refrigerator and freezer.

It can be difficult to keep track of all the factors to take into account while choosing seeds. One way to identify a particular plant is to wrap a strand of brightly colored yarn loosely around it. When it comes time to gather seed, this will help you recall which plants showed characteristics like vitality. To prevent the yarn from becoming too tight and damaging the plant as it grows, be sure to monitor it regularly. An alternative is to label plants with little stakes positioned in front of them.

Chapter 4

Seed Saving Techniques

Basics of Pollination: Self-pollination vs. Cross-pollination.

Every living thing on our planet wants to procreate. Although they don't reproduce like humans, plants nonetheless do so. We call their reproduction asexual. Seeds are produced by plants in order to reproduce. Seeds contain the genetic material required to produce a new plant.

A flower is the tool a plant uses to make a seed. There is only one way that seeds can be produced, and that is by mutual pollination between blooms of the same species. Pollination is the collective word for the process of moving pollen grains from a male anther to a female anther.

For the sake of their species' survival and expansion, all plants must reproduce. Pollination is the process by which plants reproduce. Blooms aid in the propagation of plants. The most attractive feature of a plant is its bloom, which also facilitates pollination. The process by which pollen grains produced by a flower are transferred from its anther to the stigma of another bloom, or to another flower, is known as pollination. Natural agents like birds and insects, as well as biological agents like water and wind, are necessary for this process to occur. We refer to these as pollination agents. "Pollinators" is another name for them.

An animal's inadvertent actions on a flower cause pollination. Pollen grains adhere to the pollinator's body at those moments when it consumes and gathers the protein and other nutrients from the pollen or when it is consuming the nectar from the blossom. Pollen frequently lands on the stigma of the other flower when that animal visits it, enabling the flower to reproduce successfully.

need plant diagram

Next, pollen from the anther of the first flower settles on the stigma of the second blossom. Pollen most likely germinates on the flower's stigma, where it forms a sticky "pollen tube," before moving on to grow in the plant's ovule.

The three conclusions of this growth are as follows:
- The flower has been successfully fertilized, and the seeds and fruits have begun to grow.
- It is possible that the plant is only partially fertilized, in which case the fruits and seeds may not develop to their full potential.
- As a result, the plant cannot pollinate and will not grow at all.

Pollen grains might be pollinated in two separate blooms or in the same blossom.

There are two types of pollination depending on where the pollen is transferred.

Self Pollination

Cross Pollination

We'll now examine these two pollination techniques and discuss the distinctions between cross- and self-pollination.

Self Pollination

One bloom at a time experiences self-pollination. It is the main process of pollination. Pollen grains are moved from the anther to the stigma of the same flower in this process. The procedure is simple, rapid, and easy to comprehend.

During this process, pollen grains from the anther, or the male reproductive structure of the flower, are transmitted to the stigma, or the female reproductive structure of that same flower, as well as other flowers on the same plant. Animals, the wind, or the water carry the pollen grains.

Self-pollination is practiced by plants such as orchids, oats, beans, peas, sunflowers, peanuts, peaches, potatoes, and wheat. When self-pollination occurs, gametes and eventually zygotes are formed from the genetic material of the parent plant. Therefore, plants produced by self-pollination lack genetic variety.

When a flower's carpel and stamen mature at the same time, self-pollination takes place. In order to draw in insects and birds, this technique does not require any pollination agents, nectar, or pollen.

Self-pollination can be classified into two categories: autogamy and geitonogamy.

Autogamy is the term for the transfer of pollen from one bloom to another through the stigma.

Geitonogamy is the term for the process by which pollen is transferred from one bloom to another's stigma on a single gymnosperm flower.

How does Cross Pollination occur?

A more varied type of pollination is called cross-pollination. Pollen grains are transferred from one flower's anther to another flower's stigma when this happens. The destination flower is a distinct species of flower. The rise in genetic variety is a result of this pollination technique. This occurs as a result of genetic information from many flowers being merged and mixed together. It produces progeny that are distinctive. In this instance, different plants go through the reproductive process.

Heterogamy is another name for cross-pollination. This kind of pollination involves the transfer of sperm-filled pollen grains from plant one's blossoms to the second plant's egg-bearing flowers. It can be found in plants that bear cones as well as those that bloom.

Bees and other birds and animals, as well as the wind, can all participate in cross-pollination. Insects cross-pollinate a large number of fruit-bearing plants, including tulips and daffodils, as well as flowers, including apples, strawberries, raspberries, grapes, and plums. It is possible to witness wind pollination in dandelions, maple trees, and various grasses.

Isolation Techniques to Prevent Cross-pollination.

In order to successfully save seeds that are true to type, isolation is one of three essential factors (along with population-size management and selection). Preserving a variety's distinctive qualities is crucial when it comes to seed saving. Seeds harvested from open-pollinated variants remain true to type because keeping plants of the same species apart inhibits cross-pollination. When necessary isolation distances are not achievable, inventive solutions can be employed to avoid cross-pollination between two kinds of the same species. Isolation by distance is the most reliable method of doing this.

Overview of Isolation

There are various ways to control isolation, including timing flowering, containment, and distance. The best strategy is isolation by distance, which is keeping a variety sufficiently far away from any sources of contaminated pollen to guarantee that the variety stays true to type. A species' mating strategy determines how far apart plants must be isolated in order to effectively prevent cross-pollination. For grains that pollinate themselves, like oats, this distance can be as little as 10 feet, but for crops that pollinate themselves, like spinach, it can be as much as several miles.

Distance Separation

Pollen that is unwanted can come from several places. It typically originates from other varieties of the same species that are planted nearby, such as plants in your own garden, those of your neighbors, or farms that are close by. Pollen from naturalized or native wild plants of the same species, or from a species that is cross-compatible with the one being produced for seed, is another less common source of undesirable cross-pollination, though it can still be important for some species. Remember that pollen is only exchanged by plants during blooming, thus isolation is only necessary when two or more suitable kinds flower simultaneously.

Plants that predominantly self-pollinate often need less isolation distance, whereas plants that primarily cross-pollinate typically need longer distances. Because pollen from wind-pollinated crops, like spinach and beets, is very small and light and may travel considerable distances on air currents, wind-pollinated species frequently have relatively significant isolation distances. Compared to crops pollinated by wind, crops pollinated by insects could need a little less space between kinds since insects like to collect pollen and nectar in small spaces.

The direction of the predominant wind, topography, planting size, and insect numbers in the area are other elements that affect the extent to which pollen spreads and the probability of cross-pollination. The size of both populations should be taken into account in addition to the general arrangement of plants in the landscape with respect to other cross-compatible populations. A variety's chances of wayward pollen entering the population as a whole, whether via a pollinator or the wind, increase with the number of plants in the variety. Similarly, the more cross-compatible pollen and the likelihood of unintentional cross-pollination, the more plants of the same species there are in the surrounding landscape—whether as wild plants, in neighboring gardens, or in large stands of adjacent agricultural fields.

If you save seeds from only one variation of a species at a time, you can often achieve isolation by distance efficiently. Saving seeds from one type of a crop entails cultivating only that variety if the crop is often grown for its edible fruits or seeds, as is the case with melons, okra, or sunflowers. Several cultivars can be cultivated in the same garden if the crop is usually harvested before it reaches the reproductive stage, as is the case with turnips and Swiss chard. The key is to make sure that only one variety is permitted to flower and produce seeds. Assuming that contaminated pollen won't enter from nearby farms or gardens, this method is only practical when gardeners are able to completely remove the chance of unintentional cross-pollination with plants in nearby landscapes or gardens. Saving seeds from a single variety within a species at a time makes sense because many vegetable species' seeds can last for years. Put another way, you can save your favorite cultivar of broccoli one season and your favorite kind of cabbage the next.

Hand Pollination Techniques

Hand pollination is the process of moving pollen by hand from the flower's stamen, or male portion, to its pistil, or female portion. To aid in the plant's reproductive process is the goal of hand pollination. The hand pollination techniques are determined by the plant's sexuality and the process's goal.

Shaking the plant is the most basic method of hand pollination for hermaphrodite flowers on plants. There are male and female components to these self-fertile flowers. Hermaphrodite-flowering plants in gardens include eggplants, tomatoes, and peppers. Usually, a slight wind is enough to aid hermaphrodite flowers in their sexual reproductive process. Low fruit yields and the necessity for manual pollination may arise from growing these plants inside or in a protected space like a greenhouse or walled garden.

Timing for Seed Harvesting

When harvest time comes around and all those gorgeous fruits and vegetables start to build up, gardeners find that this is the most satisfying part of the season. The handful of fruits or plants that are deliberately left on the vine to develop begin to set seed a few short weeks after the fresh harvest begins, which doubles the joy for seed savers. The reward is more than ample after a long season of organizing, growing, tending to, and harvesting the garden's produce!

Do You Have Ripe Seeds?

Knowing when the seeds they are storing are genuinely mature is the first thing a seed saver has to know. When the fruit is ready to eat, it usually isn't. As you can see, practically every vegetable we eat is a young fruit that has reached ripeness. Cucumbers, okra, lettuce, radishes, and peas are all harvested for human consumption prior to the fruits' seeds becoming fully ripe. Certain plants, such as biennial brassicas, require two complete growing seasons before they yield any seed at all.

Some plants, like beans, tomatoes, and melons, bear an abundance of fruits that are large enough for the gardener to eat some of them and yet have plenty left over for seed.

If seed is wanted, output from other crops, such as head lettuce, radishes, broccoli, and turnips, must be kept whole. Not many vegetables that we eat stay on the plant long enough to yield edible seeds, and the ones that do are frequently not very tasty. Cucumbers, for instance, are huge, yellow, and extremely tender when fully mature.

Chapter 5

Harvesting Dry Seed

The seeds that are formed in pods or on flowering stems are known as dry **seeds**. These comprise all leaf and head lettuces, all root crops, all legumes, and all brassicas (cabbage, kale, broccoli, kohlrabi, collards, etc.).

When the fruit capsules or pods start to open, or when the seeds start to change from green to brown or black, the blooming stems' seeds are ready. It is best to collect these seeds before the plant naturally scatters them, a process called **"shattering."**

If you are looking for a self-sowing vegetable such as spinach or lettuce, letting the plant break is a perfect option. Should that not be the case, you will have to gather whole stems or bunches as soon as their seeds begin to sprout, or you may separate the ripe seeds from their pods and transfer them to a bucket or paper bag.

A paper bag, feed sack, or drop cloth can be used to hold the seed heads while the entire plant is pulled out and hung on a rafter in the barn or an open shed until it dries fully. You can use any device or container that can retain your harvest and still provide adequate airflow.

When seeds for legumes start to rattle inside their pods, they are ready to be harvested. Cleaning these seeds only requires removing the seeds, winnowing the chaff, and storing them because they are already hard and nearly completely dry when ripe.

No More Chaff/Detritus

When processing large amounts of dry seed, especially when final appearance is essential, seed screens come in very handy.

Seed displays are cleverly straightforward. A metal screen that is flat is fixed firmly onto a frame made of wood or metal. Seed of various sizes can be sorted through the holes in screens due to the variation in mesh size.

Chaff and seeds are forced through the perforations in the screen or sifted on top of it. While the chaff is sometimes sorted away and the seeds are kept on top, most of the time the screen's apertures are utilized to let the seeds fall onto a tarp or other container that is waiting for them.

Threshing is another method for cleaning dried seeds. In order to release the seeds, the mature, dried pods or seed heads are pounded, flailed, or wrapped in a tarp. It might be as mild as rubbing seed heads between gloved hands, or as forceful as pounding or crushing them with a hammer or other object.The whole batch is winnowed after the seeds are liberated to separate the heavier seeds from the lighter chaff. The comparatively heavy seeds fall straight down during this process, while the lighter chaff and immature seeds fly away.

This is frequently achieved by transferring material that has been threshed from one vessel to another and letting the contents fall freely through the air that is moving very gently.

Optional techniques for winnowing include hurling the contents from a basket into the air and catching the falling seeds (which is entertaining but a little difficult at first), filtering the chaff through different-sized screens, or utilizing a tarp or board with a batten on a small incline to allow the heavier seeds to fall to the bottom while the chaff is kept in check. For home seed savers and gardeners, the preservation and functionality of the seed itself do not depend on removing all of the chaff.

Methods for extracting seeds from different types of fruits and vegetables.

Fruit-seed separation is a specialized task. In addition to its physical look, a small amount of carelessness during the extraction process can seriously harm the seed's viability and vigor. An ineffective extraction method may potentially be the cause of in-situ germination. The procedures listed below can be used to separate the seed.

1.Acid Technique

The completely ripened, mature fruits are collected using this approach, and they are then ground into pulp. The pulp is removed and the commercial HCL added to a convenient-sized plastic, wooden, or cement tub container. After fully mixing, the pulp and acid are stored for that amount of time. The acid's corrosiveness during this time dissolves the mucilage that is attached to the seed, releasing the pulp from the seed.The seeds are then properly washed four to five times in water to remove any remaining acid, as this could damage the seed's embryo. This approach allows for a faster extraction of seeds. The seeds exhibit a vivid color, strong germination, and resistance to fungal invasion. Regardless of variety, the various extraction techniques revealed that the acid procedure had a higher seed recovery percent. When soaking for 30 minutes with 2.5% HCL, germination was at its peak.

2. The Fermentation Process

In a non-metallic container, the crushed fruits are left for two to three days to ferment. Fruits should ferment for two days to produce the highest-quality seeds, according to observations. As fermentation progresses, the seeds separate from the sticky pulp and descend to the bottom of the container. To get the appropriate moisture level, the seeds are separated, carefully cleaned, and dried in the shade. In comparison to other extraction methods, there is a lower seed recovery rate. The pulp's fermentation and the fungal burden within the seeds cause the seeds to turn a drab color. Extended periods of fermentation may lead to in situ germination. Vegetables such as tomatoes, brinjal, cucumbers, water melons, musk melons, etc. are prepared using these techniques.

3. Mechanical Extraction of Seeds

Vegetables like tomatoes, brinjal, and chillies are the principal targets of this technique.In tomato, the pulpermachine is fed a known weight of matured tomato fruits. After being removed individually from the outlet, the pulp holding the seed is cleaned in water and allowed to dry in the shade. Pulpers are another tool that can be used to crush the fruits of brinjal. Adequate water is added prior to utilizing pulpers, and the pulp is well agitated after pulping. The maximum seed rate extraction (3.327 kg/hr) was achieved when using a vegetable seed extractor with a treatment combination of 2 mm concave clearance, 8.5 m/s cylinder peripheral speed, and 1.76 of feed rate per hour. When dried chilli fruits are fed into the seed extractor's feed hopper, they are beaten, separating the seeds, which then exit through the outlet. By hand, the seed and hulls separated. 96% of the seeds were extracted efficiently.

4.Alkali Method

Harvested and crushed fully ripened mature fruits are used to generate pulp. In order to speed up the fermentation process in tomatoes, 500g of 0.5% sodium bicarbonate mixed in 10 cups of warm water is added to the pulp and left for a day.Once separated, the seeds are cleaned with water to remove any remaining alkali.

5.The Citric Acid Method

This seed extraction method eliminates the gelatinous coating from seeds without compromising germination or viability by applying

30 g of citric acid to one liter of pulp and allowing the pulp to digest for two hours. However, this approach has only been found to affect tomato seed storability.

6. Acid Modified Procedure

Water is used to pulp freshly picked fruits. After removal of the pulp and pearls, the wet seed with mucilage remains. Produces 1 kg of moist seed for every 10 kg of fruit. This is mixed with forty milliliters of commercial HCL and left to react for twenty minutes while being constantly stirred. After washing, the seeds are dried. This technique preserves acidity without compromising seed quality or recovery. It is utilized in musk, watermelon, and tomatoes.

7. Dehydration Technique

The fruits are gathered when completely developed and allowed to dry for two to three days in the sun.To restore the original moisture content, the seeds are dried in the sun between the hours of 8:00

am and 11:00 am and 2:00 pm after being extracted. Examples include ridge gourds, spinach gourds, chillies, and okra.

8. Easy Harvesting Mature Pods Method

After being harvested when fully mature, the pods are sun-dried for two to three days in order to lower their moisture content to 15–16%. To minimize mechanical damage to the seeds, excessive drying and vigorous pounding should be avoided. Next, the pods are struck with a pliable bamboo stick to remove the seeds. The quality of the seed is lowered by excessive mechanical damage. Mostly used for cluster beans, okra, french beans, lablab beans, cowpeas, etc.

9. Manual Seed Extraction Method

In this method, the seeds are extracted manually after the fruits are split into longitudinal pieces. Seed remnants are dried and pulp remnants are cleaned. This process has a significant impact on seed storability as well. Examples include watermelons, muskmelon, bitter gourds, and pumpkins.

10. The Floatation Technique

Flotation technique is used to separate the sinkers and floaters. You can remove the immature seeds as floaters. Such as bottle gourds and other large seed veggies.

11. Wet Method

This approach was used for sweet pepper. After the fruits are smashed, the seeds are mechanically extracted from the remaining pulp and debris. In order to separate the seed from the detritus, the crushed material is often fed into a rotating cylindrical screen.

Chapter 6

Seed Storage

Many seeds lose half of their viability in six months when stored under regular room conditions, or open storage.

Compared to thin-coated seeds, tougher seed coats typically have longer seed lives.

Reduced seed moisture content and regulated storage temperature are necessary for better storability.

Use this easy method, step-by-step, to store seeds:

1.Store only seeds that are fresh, healthy, mature, and well-dried.

2.To prolong their life, keep them somewhere cool and dry.

3.Reabsorbing moisture is easy for seeds. Store seeds in airtight containers (such as glass jars with tight-fitting covers or tin cans) to ensure dryness.

4.Add some absorbent material for the dampness. You can use little pieces of newspaper, toasted (cooled) rice, powdered milk, dry wood ash, or dry charcoal. About 1/4 of the container should be occupied by the drying material.

5.Write the kind of seed, location, and collecting date on the containers' labels.

6.Provide the seeds' initial percentage of viability if at all possible. Start by planting some seeds and counting how many of them sprout. For example, the viability percentage is 80% if 8 out of 10 germinate.

7.You can use this information to determine the amount of viability loss that occurs in each variety of seed between collection and planting.

8.Defend seeds from fungus and insects. Mix with dry ash, black pepper powder, or neem leaf powder before storing in containers. Alternatively, use cotton, castor bean, peanut, or neem extract: 1 kilogram seed and 1 teaspoon oil. Alternately, use one or two naphthalene balls per ten kg of seed.

9.Keep birds and rats away from the storage area. Use airtight containers at all times for optimal seed storage.

Seed should be stored in glass jars, metal boxes, tin cans, plastic bags, or containers with sealable covers once it has fully dried.

When utilizing sealed containers, keep the following in mind:

- Avoid sealing wet seeds.
- Utilize airtight packaging.
- Verify the cleanliness of the container.
- Only when absolutely required, open the seed containers.

Certain species' seeds cannot withstand drying out or being too cold. These include, but are not limited to, neem, rubber, cocoa, mahogany, jackfruit, avocado, rambutan, durian, and mangosteen. Only a few days to a few months can be spent storing them in a regular room. Therefore, planting these types shortly after collection is ideal. If storage is necessary, however, do not allow the seeds dry out entirely.

- Don't dry them out too much. For a moist seed kernel, aim for a dry seed coat.

- Seed and a small amount of damp charcoal, peat moss, sawdust, or sand should be placed in plastic bags half full.

- Store the bags in a cold area.

- Allowing air to enter, open the bags for 30 minutes every day.

Labeling seeds for easy identification

In order to readily identify and arrange your seed collection for future planting, labeling your seeds properly is an essential part of seed saving. Clearly labeling seeds helps ensure efficient seed management and avoids confusion, whether you're storing seeds from your garden or taking part in a seed exchange. Here are some pointers for properly labeling seeds:

1.Utilize Durable and Waterproof Materials:

Select labels that are composed of materials resistant to rain, sunlight, and moisture from the soil. For seed labeling, weather-resistant paper or plastic that is waterproof work best.

Steer clear of fabrics that fade, rip, or otherwise degrade over time.

2. Provide Important Details:

On each seed label, clearly put the name of the plant species or variation. If applicable, provide any pertinent information, such as the name of the cultivar.

Give more information, including the date the seeds were obtained, the location of the seed collection (if applicable), and any particular growing circumstances or parent plant characteristics.

3. Make Use of Proper Printing or Handwriting:

Clear, readable handwriting or printing should be used to write or print the information on the seed label. If you want to make sure the label stays readable over time, use a waterproof pen or marker.

Use printed labels or sticky labels with pre-written information if your handwriting is hard to read.

4. Clearly attach labels to seed packets or containers:

Using waterproof glue or tape, firmly affix seed labels to seed packets, envelopes, or containers. Make sure the labels are securely attached to avoid them coming off when handling or storing. Put the label on the front or back of seed packages or envelopes, where it will be easily readable.

5. Sort Seeds in a Systematic Way:

Decide on a methodical way to arrange your seed collection, like numbering the seed lots or alphabetizing the plant types.

To keep seeds neat and accessible, store them in drawers, cartons, or other labeled containers. To keep different kinds of seeds apart inside larger containers, think about utilizing partitions or dividers.

6. Make a catalog or seed inventory:

Maintain a thorough catalog or inventory of your seed collection, including a list of all the different types of seeds you have and pertinent details like source, amount, and rate of germination.

To create and manage your seed inventory, use a database, spreadsheet, or seed-saving program. As you plant current seeds or add new ones, make sure to update the inventory on a regular basis.

7. Keep seeds and labels together:
To keep the seeds paired and easily recognized, store the seed labels with the matching seeds. Put labels inside envelopes or seed packs, or use rubber bands or twine to fasten them to containers.

8. Take Into Account Other Labeling Techniques:
To identify between various sorts of seeds or seed varieties, think about employing color-coded labels, symbols, or other visual clues in addition to written labeling.

Include barcodes or QR codes on seed labels that connect to online databases or information about the seeds to provide quick access to more details.

Make sure that your seed collection is correctly identifiable, accessible, and well-organized by adhering to these labeling requirements. Proper labeling makes managing seeds easier, encourages effective germination and cultivation, and makes seed saving a more enjoyable and rewarding process.

Chapter 7

Seed Viability Testing

Gardeners and farmers can evaluate the quality and viability of their seed stocks before planting by conducting seed viability testing, which is an essential stage in the seed-saving process. Through the process of determining the viability of seeds, people may separate out those that are no longer viable from those that are likely to germinate and grow into healthy plants. This section will go over a number of seed viability testing techniques and offer detailed instructions for carrying out tests at home.

Test Seed Viability: Why Do It?

1.To maximize germination rates and guarantee a good crop, as it is crucial to determine the viability of the seeds before planting. Over time, a number of factors, including age, storage conditions, moisture exposure, and temperature variations, can impact the viability of seeds. Growers can detect seeds with low germination rates by assessing the viability of the seed. Then, they can take the necessary actions, like increasing seed density or seed priming, to increase seedling establishment in the garden or field.

Seed Viability Testing Methods

1.Typical Germination Test:

One popular technique for determining a seed's viability is the germination test. It entails incubating a sample of seeds under carefully regulated conditions on damp paper towels or germination paper.

In order to perform a normal germination test, use distilled water to evenly dampen, but not completely wet, a paper towel or germination paper. On the paper towel, scatter a predetermined number of seeds (often 10 to 100, depending on the size and availability of the seeds).

To preserve moisture levels, wrap or fold the paper towel around the seeds and store them inside a closed plastic bag or container. Put the date, the type of seed, and any other pertinent information on the bag or container's label.

Keep the seeds warm, well-lit, and at a steady temperature that is suitable for the type of seed you are planting. Regularly inspect the seeds for germination indicators, such as the appearance of roots or the splitting of the seed coat.

Determine the germination percentage by counting the number of seeds that have sprouted after a certain amount of time (typically 7 to 14 days). This can be done by adding up all the seeds that were tested.

2.Tetrazolium Test (TZ):

The dehydrogenase enzyme activity in live seeds provides the basis for the quick and accurate tetrazolium test, which determines the viability of seeds. The process is applying a tetrazolium chloride stain on seeds, which reacts with living tissues to generate an apparent color shift. Tetrazolium chloride should be dissolved in water in accordance with the manufacturer's instructions to create a solution for a tetrazolium test. Soak a sample of seeds in the mixture, then let them sit in the dark at a particular temperature for a prearranged amount of time.

Take the seeds out of the fluid after incubation, then cut them open to look at the inside tissues. Whereas non-viable tissues stay unstained or appear white or pale, viable tissues will appear pink or red, signifying an active metabolism and the possibility of germination.

To ascertain the viability of seeds, note the proportion of viable seeds based on the color of the internal tissues.

3.Seedling Emergence Test

Seed viability is evaluated using the seedling emergence test, which involves directly planting seeds in soil or a growth medium and tracking the emergence of seedlings over time. With this approach, field conditions and environmental factors influencing germination are more accurately represented.

Use sterile growth media, such as vermiculite or potting soil, in pots or trays to prepare seedlings for emergence testing. After planting a sample of seeds at the species-recommended depth and spacing, give the pots or trays a good thorough watering.

In order to ensure that the seedlings emerge, place the pots or trays in a constantly wet, warm, and well-lit area and check them frequently. Based on the total number of seeds planted, determine the percentage of seeds that germinate by counting the number of seedlings that emerge.

As necessary, modify the planting depth, soil moisture content, and other variables to maximize seedling emergence and guarantee precise outcomes.

Interpreting the Findings of a Seed Viability Test:

High germination percentage seeds (usually 70% or more) are deemed viable and fit for planting.

Although they might still be viable, seeds with low germination percentages might need more care or treatments to increase germination rates.

Seeds that do not germinate at all or only sprout at a very low percentage are probably not viable and should be thrown away or put to other uses.

A crucial tool for seed savers is seed viability testing, which offers insightful data regarding the viability and quality of seed stocks prior to planting. Growers may increase the effectiveness of their farming or gardening projects, optimize germination rates, and save priceless seed supplies by combining testing techniques with close monitoring.

Conclusion

As our exploration into seed saving comes to an end, let us consider the deep importance of this age-old custom and its capacity to change people, communities, and ecosystems. With the knowledge and abilities you'll need to start your own seed-saving adventure, we've explored the ethics, methods, and guiding principles of seed saving throughout this book.

Seed saving is a celebration of diversity, honoring the wisdom of generations past and fostering resilience in the face of uncertainty. We support genetic diversity preservation and the protection of endangered plant kinds by preserving and dispersing seeds from a wide variety of plants.

It's also a potent instrument for fostering self-sufficiency, food sovereignty, and community engagement. Our food systems will be shaped in accordance with our values as we take back control of our seed supply.

By fostering ecological resilience and reducing the need for artificial inputs, we become stewards of the land through our efforts to save seeds. In a world filled with unprecedented challenges, such as corporate consolidation in the seed industry and climate change, saving seeds gives hope. A tiny act of resistance and a pledge to the planet's welfare is represented by each seed preserved. Your work counts, whether you run a farm or just a backyard garden. We can make a world where every seed matters, every garden thrives, and everyone has access to wholesome food that is produced responsibly.

I sincerely appreciate you journeying with me. May the joy of growing and sharing life fill your hearts, may your gardens be abundant, and may your seeds be productive.

Thank You.

Made in United States
North Haven, CT
20 May 2024

52759101R00046